THE HUGGER MUGGER

SELECTED POEMS - 2020

SEÁN HALDANE

RUNE
PRESS

For GML as always.

Published in 2020 by Rune Press Ltd, London,
England

www.runepress.com

Cover painting by Matthew Webber
Design by Peter Keighron

Printed and bound in Great Britain by TJ International Ltd.,
Padstow, Cornwall.

ISBN: 978-09574669-7-5

CONTENTS

DESIRE IN BELFAST

A COUNTRY WITHOUT NAME

MIDWINTER RACING

THE HUGGER MUGGER

TWO SONG CYCLES

SELECTED POEMS

Author's Note

My previous collections of poems have been in chronological order. But there are two chronologies: the order in which poems are written, and the order of the events they describe. For example there are six poems in *The Memory Tree* (2015) which concern events before *The Coast and Inland* (1968). I have written poems set in Italy while living in Canada, poems set in Canada while living in England. My longest collection so far, *Always Two* (2010) contains about 280 poems set in four European countries, the USA, and six Canadian provinces.

Since this is a selection, not a collection, I have felt free to organise the poems in a loose chronological order of writing, and to put together some poems which 'belong' together – whether in place, time, or person.

Some of the most recent poems have been set in song cycles by the Canadian composers James Moffet (Poems of Absence) and David Jaeger (The Echo Cycle). These appear in this collection as the last two poem titles in the book.

SELECTED POEMS

DESIRE IN BELFAST

INVOCATION

O swimming vegetables by the Smithfield market
And urine running down the legs of women
At the bus stops, O lowering hills of Belfast –
Never stop raining: sun would see too much.

O rolling in the bunkers of rained-out golf courses
In the gritty sand of our repentance,
We thank thee for thy weather, O Belfast –
Never stop raining: sun would see us bare.

And Oh our smell would come surging out of us
With no baffle of musty rain-soaked wool
To keep it in, and Oh we'd be ashamed –
Never stop raining: sun would see us flesh.

And Oh the roses would no longer grow
In McGredy's gardens, petals would fall to dust,
The thorny briars of our hearts' veins exposed –
Never stop raining: sun would see us dead.

DESIRE IN BELFAST

Hothouse of desire,
In the Botanic Gardens,
Jungle damp, steaming pipes, banana fronds.
Against the railing of the goldfish pond,
Leaning back, she pulled up her dress,
Round-bellied as a Hindu goddess.

Volumes of desire,
Behind the shelves of the Linen Hall Library,
She sitting on my knee, I reading Dante:
'He kissed my mouth all trembling'
(*La bocca mi baciò tutto tremante*).

School of desire,
Waiting for me in the park, her uniform skirt
Unbuttoned, knickers in her satchel –
We'd lie on leaves in the dirt.

Bush of desire,
Rhododendron dripping on us bare,
Blood-coloured petals caught in her hair.

Flowers of desire,
Hydrangeas in the suburbs,
'Like blue notepaper', quoting Rilke, she said.
I wrote our story in fallen hawthorn petals,
Printing it in the crushed daisies and buttercups
We made our bed.

Reservoir of desire,
Children and pensioners playing with model boats,
Us on a wrought iron bench,
Hands in each other's clothes under our coats.

Concert of desire,
At recitals or the symphony,
Thinking of afterwards – against a wall
In the dark puddles of an entry.

Journey of desire,
The last Cave Hill bus at night,
On the back seat of the empty upper deck,
My eye on the round mirror above the stairs,
Her fingernails dug into my neck.

Song of desire,
The blackbird at Island Mohee
Which brought a saint eternity,
Us among the brambles kissing,
Purple-mouthed with blackberry.

River of desire,
The Lagan, factories wrecked by Luddite time,
Gladed by nettles, burrs, thorns,
Millwheels stopped in slime,
A muddy dell, us crouching in the mire.

Hill of desire,
Woods, sheeps' paths, caves, paper and shit,
Peeping Toms... On the summit
Us lying in heather and gorse on fire.

Lane of desire,
Buttermilk Loney, where before the Twelfth
Townies dragged down branches for the bonfires
(And groped the two backward sisters
From the white, half-doored cottage),
She stepping around the cowpats
And singing 'A la claire fontaine'.

Rain of desire,
Pouring down the windows of the car
We locked ourselves in
Parked off the Hightown Road on the moors
(B Specials patrolled in Land-Rovers with Sten
guns),
Lying skin to skin.

City of desire,
Us walking hand in hand
('Stand still ye sinners!'
Bellowed at us by a soapbox preacher),
Half a million rages
Rising with the smoke from chimneys,
The air sparkling between our eyes.

Poems of desire,
Graves ('one story and one story only'),
Blake's Book of Thel, Rilke's autumn day, Goethe
Tapping hexameters on his mistress's shoulder,
Breton's woman with the woodfire in her hair –
And from me to her how Spring would pass,

May blossom shivering from the tree
Falling white on grass.

Stones of desire,
The dolmen in the Giant's Ring.
Among the chocolate wrappers
And broken bottles glistening
By moonlight, us in our blanket, trembling.

Stars of desire,
Orion ungirding his sword,
The rising Milky Way –
Sheathed in her I lay.

Coals of desire,
In January, heating a borrowed room,
Bursting frozen pipes in the attic,
Ceiling plaster falling on us naked.

Death of desire,
My disgust.
Love had turned to lust –
That sticky, tender love.
Recalled after thirty years
It brings me to tears.

PEEPING TOM

A man was standing over us.
I felt his eyes prying my buttocks apart.
Fuck off! I snarled, neck twisted to glare up at him.
He laughed but took a step back nervously
Licking his lips, then said, *How old are youse?*
Sixteen? You should be ashamed of yourselves!

I was ashamed. Of being stuck,
Unable to roll out of my girl and expose
Her to him. She grabbed her raincoat
And pulled it over us. We lay there small
Under him. *Should be ashamed*, he said.
Then, one hand in his trouser pocket,
He stumbled off into the miles of sky,
And left us on those moors ruffled by wind,
The heather flowers pink around my head.

THE BULLHEAD

Fishing where the cold and vicious tide
Swept between rocky islands, I dragged in
A bull-head, spiny, with lurid scales.
I cut it off the hook and threw it back.

That month on the same coast, changed in sun,
She and I found beaches of pure coral
And swam in that sea whose foam
Stung our bodies, quickening desire.
At evening we stepped through walls,
Lifting the stones aside with shaky hands,
To find a patch of grass and blown bog cotton
Where we could lie in shadow cast by boulders
As the sun sank and spilled its fire.

One night we ate dulse, then drank poteen. Rage
At her unfaithfulness burned in my brain.
I turned and staggered, shoved her to the ground.
Then we walked back together in cold shame.

Next day we crossed by boat to Inishmore,
She gaily singing to the other men,
And when we climbed to Dun Aengus fort
I muttered to myself I'd smash her head
On the sharp teeth of the chevaux-de-frise:
Each spike of stone went straight into my heart.

Desperately I tugged her behind the wall

Of the fort and pulled her to the grass,
Begging her to hold me. She refused.
Then we all lay together on the cliff
Three hundred feet above the emerald sea.
I felt myself vertiginously dragged
Close to the edge, while she talked happily
And flirted with my friends, taking one's hand
And reading in the lines. I'd nothing to say.
I didn't belong up on the sunny land:
No more that spiny fish, my jealousy.

She wept in silence when I turned away.

YES, RAGE

Rage to get the moment back,
Smash your knuckles till they crack
Against the wall of stone, smack
Your head upon the chevaux-de-frise,
Grovel on your muddy knees,
Dribble grief onto the sod,
Stuff your pizzle in a clod,
Shriek to seagulls or to God,
Crack your nails down to the quick
Tearing at your shrunken prick,
Rage to get the moment back,
In mind's eye spiral through the black
To where she lies and dies in wrack,
Lashed, splashed and battered on the strand,
Cast over cliff top by your hand,
She clawed the puffins from their nests
And scraped the white skin off her breasts,
Slithered down the gullies, down
To crash in pounding wave crests, drown…
You lack the guts to throw yourself
After her from this towering shelf,
So howl and lacerate your pelt
And clutch and thump and wail your woe
While she dies where you dare not go –
Yes, rage to get the moment back.

NOTES

What duets we played on the violins of us!
What thrills from our organ flute pipes! How full-bel-
lied
The throbbing from our tympani, how melodious
The strains from our oboe d'amore, our ophicleide!

Now our music room is locked up, silent with dust,
Our instruments abandoned. Mice have eaten the glue
Of the violins, the wood is rotting, and rust
Eats the metal where spittle ran in the winds we blew.

How sad this lack of any sound except the mice
Occasionally pattering among things not nice.

All that is left of the double concerto we played
Is notes: minims, black crochets and quavers, in bars
I scribble on old paper. The music we made
Is lost on its long journey to the stars.

THE BLACKBIRD

(The italic lines are a version of the medieval Irish poem *Int én bec*, known as 'The Blackbird of Belfast Lough.')

The entry where we courting stood
Is stained with lovers' blood.
Across the Bog Meadows, bombs
And bullets break flesh for tombs.
The red buses we used to burn
Inside are charred with real fire.
The pub's become a funeral pyre.
My dear, our childish moans
Were nothing to the groans
Of death.
                    Do not return
Unless as ashes in an urn
For scattering in that country.
The grimy walls of that entry
Are blown to dust, cobblestones
Dashed with bones.
                    Do not return
If there's one granule left to burn.

But remember the hills
Where clasped as one we'd view
The land, the great city below,
Pink terrace houses row on row,

The chimney stacks of mills,
The cracks of streets and entries –
Pottinger's, Joy's – the gantries
Looming on Queen's Island, bridges
To County Down's green ridges,
The Lagan's silver arm, the Lough.

See as we saw them in our day
The whins, the hawthorns where we lay.
Hear as we heard –

> *A small bird*
> *Whistling piped*
> *From sharp beak*
> *Pure yellow,*
> *Casts a cry*
> *On Loch Laig,*
> *Black from twig*
> *Heaped yellow –*

And let the winds from the Atlantic
Tamed by the Sperrins to pulsing air
Ruffle your hair.
Think of me: it's not so long.
I listen to the same blackbird's song.

SELECTED POEMS

A COUNTRY WITHOUT NAME

BELLOSGUARDO

How many children were conceived or born there,
How many girls and women loved or raped
In dream or deed, how many a nightmare
In the touch of skin caressing skin escaped,
How many awakened by shafts of golden light
Piercing the piously narrow window-slit,
How many haunted as dusk turned to night,
The slugs' traceries of slime moonlit
Silver on walls of flaking stone,
The cypress lonely as I, now, without you,
The olives skeletal against the moon.
We in that ancient room did nothing new.
How many others, like us (the owls hooting outside)
In sleep, in love, in fear shuddered and cried.

A COUNTRY WITHOUT NAME

In a country without name the princess lies
Beneath the stones and grass with gentian starred,
On slopes below the pending avalanche,
The gentian tubers rooted in her eyes.

She dreams of violated rooms, doors shattered,
The crenellations vitreously melted
By thunderbolts, the faces bled and blanched
Of men-at-arms in pieces struck and scattered.

And now insects invade the sanctuary
Her thighs once guarded chaste as statuary,
They pry within her chamber and unmake
The pillars of her lost virginity.

And now the snow-shrouds trickle into flood,
And men-at-arms begin to twitch awake,
Their blackened fingers locked on rusty swords,
The brown soil crumbling in a stream of blood.

The princess moves, she breathes, her nipples rise
Like new pink buds, the earth and grass divide.
Slowly she stands upright, then horrified
Invokes the flowers of springtime to appease

The raised and trickling swords above her head:
She promises the gentians of her eyes,
The snowdrops of her skin, the buds, and last
The dusky hellebore between her thighs.

Enfolded, one by one, each warrior dies.
The flowers burst, the avalanches boom,
And she returns enshrouded to her tomb.

HERE IT'S THE MOUNTAINS THAT KILL

'Qui sono le montagne che uccidono'.
La Donna del Lago Giovanni Comisso

When you think of that country, remember
Not the ancient squares of the valley town,
Nor the paintings in its galleries.

Don't try to make the contrast clear
Between Southern slopes green with vines
And Northern, forest-dark,
Joined by summits and the pass we lived in.

Think of essential things. Crumbling trenches
Grass covered long ago, but at the inn
Hard-drinking people sing at night
Of bursting shells and broken hearts,
The Alpini songs of the Great War.

Think of their loneliness. Most people there
Have a sunless side, like the mountains.

Here it's the mountains that kill.
When we arrived the rescue team was out
Picking up the corpses of a family
Whose motor cart had crashed over the edge
Of the road in a sudden landslide.

Houses were burned in the Second War
And families were shot. (The locals
Hid partisans in the forests.)

What crime there is is violent,
Encouraged by the local brandy,
Distilled with gentian roots.

Remember the crocuses, the sun on the peaks,
The last snow patches melting near the house
Our love was dying in, that mountain Spring
When all but we proved adequate to growth.

PRIVEL DA CRAPPA!

One thing falls from another – like falling rocks:
The signs PRIVEL DA CRAPPA! caught in the head-
         lights
As we careened down forest roads from the Stelvio
(DANGER OF ROCKS!) We lay that night
Chastely back to back in a single bed.
We had first kissed the week before, as meteors fell
Over olive groves and cypresses – Notte di San Lorenzo.

Tonight is San Lorenzo. I've been reading a book
About Rumantsch: PRIVEL DA CRAPPA!
I'm using the pepper grinder I bought in Florence
That summer we came together without coming,
Not knowing all would come to nothing

And we would fall hurtling down the bends
Of time screaming without a sound.

What would we live? – lust
Falling out of love. But when did we fall in?
Were we not just good friends?
Wasn't that the trouble?
What were the fragments in the eventual rubble?
Lust, friendship, hope? It was hope
That drove us down that perilous slope.

No meteors now: the night sky is dull with haze
And we are living out our days
On separate continents. The peppercorns are ground,
Fall to dust.

AEQUOREA AEQUOREA

I think of details: *Aequorea Aequorea*
Jellyfish, iridescent in San Juan Sound.
The vibrant green/pink shafts of the aurora
In Quebec when the snow on the ground
Squeaked underfoot. The scallop-shaped aura
Green/ pink around the rising Wurlitzer organ
At the Ritz in Belfast in the 1950s.

I don't like arguments, theories:
'Women are this. Are that.' I think of the woman
I lived with on the mountains above the Piave.
I nuzzled my face in her brown wavy hair,
But we never pulsated like *aequorea aequorea*.
We sent out no light shafts, no radiant gloria.
With her, love was always *terre a terre*.

NOTHING IN PARTICULAR

I remember particulars: columbini
And crocuses where we lay on the grass,
At night the mournful songs of the Alpini
From the inn echoing across the pass.

'*There's something wrong with you,*' she said.
(This was in a fight, before we parted.)
'*You only like making love outside
In forests, on slopes – not inside, normally.*'

'*But remember when we'd do it on the floor
Beside the pot-bellied stove, at Croce d'Aune,
When the bedroom was too cold. That was inside.*'

'*Yes, and Pietro* [the landlord] *knocked on the door
And walked in on us. You embarrass me.*'

'*You're too easily embarrassed.*'

At the end of it
We lay apart in sheets like wastes of snow
Under a black sky with not a star.

We had frozen, she and I, never to soak
Into the soil of Spring. Unlike the cesspool
(In winter, from the closet's wooden O
New turds plopped onto a brown sheet of ice),
We did not thaw. The mess would not have been nice.

We could laugh at the shit. Or when I played the fool.
But nothing remained. Nothing in particular.
Life had become a sort of general joke.

BY THE RIVER OTTER

Was it the last time we were happy
Or the first time we were sad?

It tightens my heart
After almost half a century apart,
To be near the river where we struggled
Through brambles to the bank – more like a marsh
('Not very riparian, the Otter'), and I started to
explain
I forget what, but it caused you pain.
Your eyes were darker with tears,
And your voice was not like yours, it was harsh,
As you told me of your fears.
Later in bed we lay,
You in your creamy night-dress, and snuggled.
We had our way.

THE WAY OF ALL FLESH

She met me in her yellow dress
And underneath the navy blue of night –
Silk under linen, silk over skin –
She let me in,
Then afterwards, naked in bed,
She looked me in the eye and said:
'I don't want you to hurt me again.'
'I won't', I swore.

But of course I did.
I didn't know what I had
Until I had it no more.
All gone:
Her dress yellow as the sun,
Her dark blue underwear
And everything we were,
Each naïve wish –

Gone the way of all flesh.
'Ah yes – to death', the reader nods –
But no:
To other flesh as others let us in
To darker worlds than either knew
When she wore that yellow dress
And swayed like a flower
In the breeze of my love for her –
Still fresh.

A MATTER OF TIME

She loved me. I loved her. It ended. Now
One eye hides behind a leaf, the other
Stares from photocopy pigment soot.
Is she alive? The repro doesn't tell.
There's no fragrance in a Xerox smell.

A Xerox of a Xerox of a Xerox.
Irradiated love. By what nerve gas,
What blastless neutron warfare was it killed?
So wails the lover lost and losing: I.
Toxins and X rays de-marrowed my bones
And weakened muscles like a fluorescent.
Inside myself I pulled her down to hell,
Not outside on those crushed glades of bluebell,
Not in that cold dawn when she came to bed
And gave me one last time the flower I'd bled.

Gone (click), gone (click), gone (click), gone (click)
Gone (click)…
Layers of Xerox back in time's machine,
It ended. No. Gone (click). I ended it.
As love it started. I made it obscene.
And now I try to make a Xerox clean.

SELECTED POEMS

38

MIDWINTER RACING

WHAT WOMEN DO

Cosí fan tutte: so all women do.
But when I was thirteen I wasn't sure
What they did. In the opera they fell
For army officers. Divine duets
Vibrated in the Salzburg night air.

In front of me was a little Austrian girl
With serious eyes and straight brown hair.
We never spoke. I thought of her as Suzanne
When I remembered her (and I did),
Still not sure what women do.

In Vienna I saw *Tannhäuser*
In the over-heated, over-gilded Staatsoper.
A woman sitting next to me was blue,
Literally, and smelt of some sickening scent,
To cover dying, I supposed.
A soprano shrieked from a papier-mâché hill:
The Venusberg. Her fat, veiled body quivered.
Was this what women do?

Wagner wrote music – swelled with fame,
Inhaling his mistress's scented handkerchief
As he set out words and notes: the Master.
Music wrote Mozart – to death,
Coming through him in coaches and in taverns,
Forcing his cramping fingers to write it down.

Rolling with fever in summer nights in town
While his sweet Costanza played tricks at the spa
With her army officer, Mozart knew
What women do.

Sweet Suzanne of the serious eyes,
Do you remember me when you hear
Così fan tutte? So all women do –
And all men too:
We disappear.

THE DIVINE IDOT

Those dreams when I am hurled about a room,
Thudding and bouncing from the concrete walls;
When I look in a clear mirror and see my face
Purple, swollen and shining, scarified –
And suddenly the mirror dulls with mist,
Cracks and shatters fragments to the floor.

Those dreams when I talk with noble birds,
Their feathers glowing turquoise and aquamarine,
Who fly only to me, so I can bless them,
Sitting upon a throne, raised from my trance –
The fit in which I fell – by a company
Of gay yet wistful girls and boys who say:
'You are not sick, we reverence you, Friend.
You have fought the desperate red giant,
Hopelessly splintered slats on his rock-hard head.
What matter that the murderer still lives?'

Those dreams are given life by opposites
Condensed in one bright vision. I must remember
That if there were no buzzing in my head,
No hideous vibration to make me scream,
I never would be placed upon that throne:
A divine idiot, loved by women,
Though somehow differently from other men.

WHY DID I LIE?

Why did I lie
When you asked why
My love was not warm still?

I answered so
As not to show
A coldness that could kill.

Is it too much
To label such
As lost integrity?

Could it be true
That loving you
I lied more easily?

PURE CONCENTRATION

Pure concentration is a camera lens
Held just above a stream, freezing branches
And the slow ripple of the current's flow
As surely as with ice.

Through concentration you can imagine
Just for a moment – while nature perseveres
In its slow motion of change –
Your soul in a hole inside your body,
The hollow centre of a flame,
A nothing mimicking the outer form.
Pure concentration
Is cold as your soul, and dead
As an old photograph.

It's only in a trance of moving thought
That your mind can keep apace
With the warm and turbulently changing earth
As words follow each other like cells
Floating in your brain.

Don't fix things, or your brain will cease to move
And you might as well have a stone in your head.
Let your brain live in your body's flow,
The cells, the shifting electric charges.

Let your mind go with your body when it feels
The warm insides of nature. Never forget
Your brain itself is flesh.

MIDWINTER RACING

My heart raced towards its pounding finish,
My brain light as a cross country skier
On the lunging skis of my body
As it surged up and over the leaps
Between long rhythmic pacings.

Then I lay perfectly still.
I didn't want to move, but my mind
Went wandering: perhaps a spark
From your inner hearth had passed to me.
Or had it passed from me to you?

Outside I sawed wood for an hour,
Then waxed my skis and set off
On another race. My eyes streamed,
My face glowed under my woollen mask.
Ice breathed into my lungs puffed out in plumes.

At twenty below the spark was still alive,
And when I came back to you it burned
Somewhere deep in me. Our casual kiss
Was of two fires lit from the same brand –
And neither knew which way the flame leapt first.

KILLDEERS

Dead beetles that the spade upturns awake
In resurrection after winter sleep.
Every layer of life is on the move,
From deepest worms to geese migrating North.
In the woods partridge drum their wings.
Winnowing snipe zigzag and craze the sky.

Then plovers from the marsh scream out *Killdeer!*
Killdeer! We brood in silence on the time
When we'll lie beetle-like under the earth
But never rise. There's nothing positive
Between us, no least faith that we might live.

EMBER DAYS

Love took possession slowly as disease,
And blindness came upon me gradually
As your flaws of complexion and of character
Faded. Not that I replaced them with false images
In my mind. Simply, they were consumed by fever.

So when, on September evenings, I come home,
Light the barbecue, drink wine on the porch,
Waiting for heat to incandesce the grill,
And I miss you – part of a long absence, not knowing
Who is with you or where you are – I can't say
I deceive myself with an ideal.

The blindness of my love for you is real
As the invisible flame which reduces charcoal
To ember and ash. It seems the barbecue
Burns under my ribs, in lack of you.

SKINDIVING

Two swims in one afternoon: the first in you,
And now, cold as I flipper down,
Clicking noises in my ears, in the lake.

I turn from rising gravel, weeds and mud,
Toward a rippled, burnished mirror
Copper and gold around a liquid sun.

I rise through clouds and layers of colour –
Gold-brown motes... green... blue... grey –
Then pop out spluttering beside the boat.

I clamber to you over the gunwale.
On the sun-reflecting water
We gently float.

A damp stain on your bathing suit
Reminds me that you hold more lunar rhythms
Than any landlocked flood.

MOON-WORLD

I swim in a moon-world – thousands of bubbles
On my body glisten like asteroids,
Each murky pit in the lake bottom a crater,
Fish drift in squadrons like space-ships,
My hair trails behind me like the tail of a comet
In layers of silver light transmuted
By the change of element from air to water,
The cold around me like the cold of space,
The floating weeds phosphorescent as galaxies –
A world where movement is perpetual,
Where an invisible wave I stir might travel
Far out of sight to flutter the gills of a fish,
A radiation against the membranes
Of the living (who later gently rot
In the black decay of death in the mud,
Or drift as corpses above the gravel
Where eggs have been laid and burst from):
A world as if opposed to mine
But part of me (in my own body the liquid –
Behind the membrane swelling and pushing,
Containing as many creatures as the lake,
Stirring up as many nightmares,
As many hidden dividings of cells – myself
Merely a wall of consciousness
Between two living flows.)

INSIDE

Striated like the inside of a shell
Snow lies against our windows, blizzard gusts
Fill in the shovelled paths to our doors.
We're cut off, but we're not lonely here.

The smell and feel of life drift in our rooms,
Our cushions, bedspreads, carpeted floors
Are orients of colour, and though our walls
Are cold to the touch, their outside surface frost-
ed,
We move inside them full and pulsing as hearts.

Our house is a shell in a sea of billowing snow
Whose fish are birds in kelp-trees in the storm,
Whose prowlers of the deep are wolves
In a seaweed forest whose innermost lair
Is crannied as coral, glistening as mother of pearl.

I MEANT TO TELL YOU

I meant to tell you about the cracked birches
Bent double to the ground,
Iced over as if glassed around.

I meant to tell you about the snow
Crushed beneath my skis,
But then my breath began to freeze.

I meant to tell you…

ACROBATS

Snow whirls around my ankles in a gust
Of wind sweeping across the icy crust.
I cannot cry your name, it is too far.
Let the message from my frozen feet go through
My boots then crusts of ice and earth and spar
Thousands of molten miles then out to you
And up through your bare feet before I fall:
We are unwilling acrobats on this ball.

LAKE-FISHING

Blue herons rise above the hemlock firs
Of their island as we roar past, and circle,
Legs dangling, a few gaunt mothers last to leave.
As we veer away we look back down our wake
At them settling again, then chug back and forth,
Our exhaust polluting the water, trolling
For lake trout. I hook one. It pulses on the line,
Splashes beside the boat. My friend nets it.

I take the heavy fish in both hands
And bash its head on the gunwale. Blood spatters,
Then it twitches in the bow. Each catch is 'christened'
With a slug of rum-and-coke. We're tipsy
As we turn back at dusk, but haul in a pike
Which snaps at my fingers as I stun it.

The V of foam behind us becomes luminous
And the hemlocks on the shores blacken
Against an indigo sky. At the dock,
We can hardly see to gut the fish. Their heads
Fall phosphorescent through the water.

In the clubhouse, more booze at the bar.
I imagine those fat paunches in trousers
Are fish-belly white. If I slit them with my knife,
What kind of guts would roll out? A mass
More stinking than pike-offal, the innards
Of killers who never kill. Watch the look

In their eyes as they buy each other drinks,
Watch them skirt around trouble – no pike
In the weeds could be more stealthy. What sort
Of fight would they put up on a hook?
No pulsing on the line, just a long cranking
Of dead weight. No flapping in the boat –
A whimper, floundering, a rush of puke.

Their women are at home, 'fishing widows',
Fat on their stale nests, playing bridge.
If they were herons, they'd be too torpid
To rise and circle. And if they were fish?
Imagine the dried-up roes, grey fat in their sides –
But we'd never see them, they'd never take a bait.

Quick, take another drink, Men. And Women,
Keep your seats, lay out another card.
In the fishy jungles of your minds
Among the weeds there may still be some tremors,
And vertigo from glimpsing light above,
But while the bottom seethes, calm the waters,
Not to feel it: you can let the corpses
Accumulate down there, the pain is gone,
And in the jungle only the descent
Of silt, and slime forming on weed and bone.

When our minds' lakes are stilled, all to be seen
Is sky-reflecting blue, though sounds betray
Us, of mosquitoes rising from the rot
That breeds them, whining at the end of day,

And frogs whose every slow and laboured croak
From the mud anticipates our final choke.

RAGES

They were terrible years,
Although I didn't say so:
Begun in hopes and fears,
But – when I'd turned the pages
Of that book of images –
Ended in hopes and rages.

From the dying woods
Foxes came one by one,
As if emissaries,
At a wavering run,
With strings of saliva
Slobbering from bared teeth.

I'd rush to get my gun,
The old wartime 303,
And hastily I'd shoot them,
Then, wearing rubber gloves,
Inter the blood-flecked things.
There were worse buryings:

I had to shoot Louis –
My hound with the fleur-de-lys
(A marking on his brow) –
Mauled by a fox, and Jenny
The poodle (a stray I'd found).
I put them in the same ground:

A knoll above the creek,
Unflooded in the Spring,
Their graves the ones with stones,
Among the skunks and foxes —
The kind of carrion
Louis had liked to roll on.

There, by the end of August
Corn and squash were frost-blacked.
In the winter of the year,
At fifty below zero,
Apple and pear trees cracked –
Like gunshots in my brain:

An echo chamber
With floors of crazy camber,
Its matter criss-cross tracked –
Blood-spots on sheets of snow
Where wolves of angry pain
Hunted my past's poor deer.

LETTER FROM NEW IRELAND

BAIE DES CHALEURS

1

Boats are locked in the harbour, ribs cracked by the ice.
How can I breathe, how can I not breathe in your arms?

The mouths of lobster pots are smothered by snow.
How can I breathe, how can I not breathe in your arms?

As a child you skated on the ocean marbled white.
How can I breathe, how can I not breathe in your arms?

Your look is cold as these gusts bringing tears to my eyes.
How can I breathe, how can I not breathe in your arms?

But I know what moves under this snow-tongued waste of ice:
Shoals, eddies, tendrils of anemones. You emerge
From dazzling waves in summer with diamonds and pearls
On your shoulders, hair as darkly curled as seaweed,
Eyes bright as rare black jet among the pebbles.

How can I not breathe in your arms?
2

You come on skis out of the setting sun
Toward me in a gold halo.
Your shadow lunges forward across the snow.
Your eyes are darker than your shadow.

3

Let me off this frozen sea onto the frozen land
Across the salty slush and drifts that hide the frozen
sand
To where the heads are falling off the snowmen in the
thaw
And spruces stretch themselves to snap their mana-
cles of ice
As I stretch out to you in clouds of breath my melting
hand.

4

The bay thaws: cloud grey, drizzle grey, water grey,
Floes white, mist above a snowy point white,
Seagulls on the floes white and grey –
A film of white and grey.

I thaw with the sea in your arms.

In an old colour film you are belle of the ball,

Of graduation, Christmas *réveillon* –
Erect, high-cheekboned, an Indian princess,
Slow but with moments of quickness.

I move with the sea in your arms.

Your sudden smile, a flash of the sun,
Lights up the world: there is no cloud,
You are as dazzling as the summer sea
And sparkling as the tumbling waves.

I pound with the sea in your arms.

LETTER FROM NEW IRELAND

To Martin Seymour-Smith

October. Still the yellow butterflies
Dawdle around the yellow dandelions.
Asters like nebulas of Venuses
Drift in the field. Propeller search planes drone –
Like Lancasters returning to Belfast
After the war. The airmen here wear green
And hate it. As in that artsy poem by Frost,
This soft morning was mild etc. Am I obscene?
I've found my femme fatale. My thinning hair
Reveals the scar I got that otherwhere
(I smashed the windscreen when an A30
Hit black ice on the Malone Road, then a tree).
I'm not unhappy. Under this green sod
Perhaps a home awaits. If there's a God
He's in me (so I feel, without disproof
Until I take the thunderbolt of truth).
'Dog is God backwards', my daughters say,
'Dad can bark like a dog.' I'll have my day,
Then under dandelion-dappled sky
Of aster blue, a sleeping dog I'll lie.
My youngest climbed the shed roof in the garden
To pick some pears and told us 'They taste golden'.
Son of a bitch, I could be, but I think I'm
The last in the New World to bark in rhyme.
Here they pronounce Dad 'Dead'. A woman said,
'Whenever he was dronk he'd lay in the bid

61

And roar. Oi always loved moi Dead.' I like
It here. Maybe in time we'll go back West.
All the best –

PS The postal workers are on strike.

YOU AND ISLAND

You land, wind-bitten, blood-rusted
Earth ice-crumbled, shores wave-eaten,
Time against you – you'll outlast men
(Thus me) but will be outlasted
By continents whose snow-peaks shine
In sun. Once under sea, you rose,
Will sink again, and (who knows?)
Rise pink in an age far from mine,
Small hills enough for children's suck,
Curved beaches open to the salt-chuck –
Sky, sea and little land (you and
Island), breakers dying on your strand.

MAN

On the point, a man, the foresight of a gun,
Bisects the orange of the setting sun.
His shadow strikes a black line on the sand,
Cut at the neck by the next rusty headland.
Wild rose and clover scents in his nose
Mingle with other smells he'd rather lose.
Naked, though not so clean, as a baby
He'll plunge into the shimmering sea
Perhaps to be reborn as more than I
To face the lemon moon, the cold sky.

WAVES

I swim through waves of pearly-everlasting,
Hollows of grass – timothy, vetch, clover,
Cobwebs' lacy nets, plashes of goldenrod –
Then gasping climb surf mountains whose snow-
crests
Topple on my head and plunge me into dark –
Howls in my ears like panic in the woods,
A naked flight through fireweed – then out to sky
And loss, loss, loss. Better to hold it in –
Pain, confusion – without her, better dead
Than waves of flowers breaking through old skin.

COUSINS SHORE

Bury me by Cousins Shore
In sand my head to cover
When I will be no more
And loose my soul to hover
(If I have one) and face
As dead chiefs used to do
(I a dead thing) the North,
The sapphire Gulf where terns
Plummet and splash, whose spray
Will sweep my ghostly vapour
Across the marram grass,
Dunes, poison ivy, roses,
Ditches hemmed with Queen Anne's lace,
To settle, baneful dew,
On fields of carnal clover –
Unless my soul, alone,
Undrownable in eyes
For which my flesh once died,
Will live as death, a sense
(No, Donne, death never dies)
Of something frightening
To couples under blankets
For skin-warmth snuggling,
The sand between their toes,
Pink sand of Cousins Shore
That oh how pleasantly
Has cleaned my flesh from bone
The couples may discover:

At dusk it gleams sepulchral
But will in time like shell
Be sand, long lost my voice,
The fleeping of a plover
Swerving quickly to skim
The waves around my head
Bobbing as alone I swim
Here in the sea, rejoice
That I am not yet dead.

SUNSTRUCK

To my father, Major Desmond Haldane, who
fought in the Reconnaissance Corps of the
51ˢᵗ Highland Division at Alamein and after.

Dead crabs (burned out tanks in desert wars)
Spongy mats of dried salt-frosted eelgrass,
Razor-clam shells, quahogs, mussels – no spoors
Of animals, but arrow tracks of birds,
A plastic bucket, a 7-Up bottle,
Streaks of guano, two dead skate gull-gutted,
Sandpipers scuttling hunch-backed at the brink,
Out in the bay at least two hundred
Canada geese honking like Gabriel hounds,
A new V landing, tails down (bombers),
Posts along the dunes (chevaux-de-frise)
To stop them drifting (camouflaged bunkers),
The (bayonets) marram grass…

                           I saw all these,
But when I doubled back around the spit –
To waves and waves of air above the waves –
My shadow leapt out sharp in front of me:
I had thought I was alone, but sun-struck
He had dogged me all along the inner shore,
And now he streaked along the strand, briskly
Dipping his head in the breakers' foam
(At a rifle pace, one hundred and twenty
A minute, a demobbed soldier) heading –
To fresh-flowered sheets, or a rumpled bed?
To welcome or disdain from her? – for home.

MI'QMAQ

Mouth like a bow, eyes angular like arrows,
Face like a heart, teeth like the white cemetery
Slabs rain-spit above the wind-torn narrows,
Breasts like the war memorial cairn's round
Stones, high laugh like a gull's (in cloud-mist) cry,
Brown hair dark-streaked like December ground
Muddy between the frosts. The memory
Of other islands in another sea
Draws me away from her. Mouth like a bow
And back tensed like a bow, her aim's not me.
Soon the sheets of rain will turn to snow.

THE MURMUR

The murmur has become a shout:
Let me out, out out!
The beating has become a din
Of hellish klaxons under skin,
The heart in its little room
Bursting in a bloody tomb
Of macerated bits of pain –
Not again, again, again.

I did this to you, my chest
Once one to one on your breast
Removed a world away – gone,
You left there, heart cracking bone.
The murmur has become a shout:
Let me out, out, out
To you my love who hurt me so
Again you've let me go.

I let you go and like a stone
I dropped over the horizon
Away from sunset-bloodied West
From you I said I loved best.
My murmur has become a shout:
Let me out, out, out.
My flown-back bird has found its nest,
I hear your heart through your breast,
My murmur has become a moan,
Let me home, home, home.

QUINCE

1

Who is the brown man raking leaves,
The russet camouflage-man who wades
As if harvesting kelp in rusty billows?
Who is the quince woman in yellow
Who rescues the aromatic fruit
From trampling under his boot,
For jelly or for marmalade?
Is he good for her or bad?
He unnerves her by day, she dare
Not turn her back or he'll jump her
As he does at night, treading, lost
In scent of crushed quince, her tree bare,
Wet with dew by dawn become a frost.
Who is the quince woman who grieves?
Who is the brown man raking leaves?

2

Who could have guessed the thorny quince
Whose golden fruit, though good for jam,
Puckered our lips and made us wince
Would, shrivelled on the bough, become
So hard, so sure, each wrinkled pome
(The one you gave me as a talisman,
An aromatic nut or stone)

Seeming eternal, and that next year
After the winter stripped it bare
The tree would throw its limbs open
With blossom so like your lips, crimson
And mauve with the rush of new blood,
The stamen pushing through its tiny hood?

LOVE'S ALPHABET

WORDS TO SAY

There are things louder than words can say.
Not to say them is your way.
There are things softer than words can say.
Not to say them is your way.
I want you to say them anyway.

I hear the thumping of your heart.
I hear the soughing of your breath.
These are louder than words can say.
These are softer than words can say.
I want you to say them anyway.

Say where I stand, where you are with me,
Whether you love or you don't love me.
These are things louder than words can say.
These are things softer than words can say.
I want to hear them anyway.

Between your breasts I press my ear.
All there is to hear I hear,
Though heart may falter, mutter, skip. . .
I place my finger on your lip,
And feel your breath against its tip.

Waves are roaring in my ear,
Our skin sings like a thousand wings
Of swallows plunging through the air,
I hear the creaking trees of your hair

Swept by the wind of words to say.

There are things louder than words can say.
Not to say them is your way.
There are things softer than words can say.
Not to say them is your way.
I hear you say them anyway.

LOST FOR WORDS

My lovely lost for words, I give you mine.
When you smile your cheeks are like apples,
Your eyes crinkle like sunshine.
When we come through moving flesh
The physical becomes a mesh
Of spirit. When you are sad,
I have one choice: repent or go mad
With remorse – again-bite of my sin
At turning from you lovely lost for words to ask me in.

AGAINST TIME

Found within membrane since we were conceived,
Against time is against me, against you –
Schism from time's flow wrongly grieved.

Against time is your opening to me,
Our breathing lip to lip, the matrix
Moulding me within, man's creatrix.

Against time are the mountains of the land
Forced upwards where volcanoes' magma reached
For mother sun, the rocky mantle breached.

Against time is our voyage on the sea
Past islands where the settlers consecrate
Small fir-hewn churches, bulwarks in time's spate.

Against time is this moment of our flesh
As fire consumes the fir logs on our hearth
To ash and charcoal staining dark the earth.

UNTIME ME

Untime me and untie me, wrench me free,
Let spinning poems cast across time's sea
Skip wave to wave as others' dead words sink
From disappearing splashes by the brink.
Grasp the tight knot between my shoulders,
Crack me crablike on the hard truth's boulders,
And where you set me gently with your hand
I'll burrow, naked hermit, in the sand.

Untime me from myself, love wrench me free
From my birthdate in this dread century:
Ack-ack, tanks outside the old house rumbling,
Walls of pink and mauve brick slowly crumbling.
Pry out with your sharp nail my coiled mainspring,
Pick inside my case and stop at nothing
Until I am two hands spread out, face open:
If I will be untimed I must be broken.

Untime me, timely snatch even my soul
And tug it with you into a black hole...
Then when primeval dreams have prowled and fed
Like dinosaurs on our flesh lying in bed,
We shall awake and rise, a new epoch
Begin, as yet untimed by any clock.
But then we'll have no time! Give time to me,
I'll give you mine, entime you, entime me.

THE ALLEY

In this alley many have come
And passed a night or two.
The walls are slippery where they lay,
The bums who snored the darkness through.

And if this is my only way to you?

THANK-YOU NOTE

My birthday present. You. I unwrap you,
Untie the ribbons, open up the gift:
All you. For me. I speak to you in tongues,
A church spire teeters in iridian skies
The sun leaps through, snow flowers on the hedges,
The wrapping torn like petals on the bed.
In your hair I bury my bald head.

THIS AND THAT

This needs that
But this this,
This that more
Than this or
That must be
You and me,
This in that
Come to this
O that this!

But for what
Does that that
That is you
Need this this?
That round this
Come to that
O this that!

SNAKES ALIVE

With sucking noises, snakes alive
In mudholes wriggle, squirm and thrive.
With rubbing noises, newly bare
Boughs test the winds of November.
With squelching noises in your blue
Raincoat, black stockings and boots, you
Cross puddles, leave the memory
Of sucking, rubbing, squelching in you me.

LOVE'S ALPHABET

My love opens to me
An M, containing V,
Embracing, thigh to thigh,
As P, become an I,
Moves up from below
Into a slippery O.

Her knees up in a Z,
Her hand stroking my head,
I lie crutched in a Y
Murmuring I will die,
The X of her and me
Now deepened to a T,
Between two D's I splay
Curved forward in a J,
Into a sideways B,
My hands around a C.

We leave the angled hell
Of E, F, K, and L,
The world of R, of U,
G, H, Q, W.

V filled, upside down A,
All letters melt away
But undulating S,
A wave of timelessness:
Our bodies since they met
Reform love's alphabet.

CONVERSATIONS

CONVERSATION ON THE PORCH

'I live with you and yet I miss you.'

'I've been far away.'

'Let me hold you then, and kiss you.
Like you to me last night
The tulips flare to day,
But now (like them to dark) you close to daylight.
Look at the chestnut candelabras –
The sets of seven leaves
Around each candle celebrating summer.
You're still bare
As when the snow came in November.'

'I don't know where
I belong. Je me sens perdue, tu sais.
What's the point?'

'Respect life in oneself and in the other.'

'Of course. I know at least the second part:
I'm a mother.
But what, finally, is there here for me?'

'Have you no heart?'

'Don't worry, don't take me seriously.
If not this, then some other thing
I'd whine about.'

'Your lips in bed last night clipped me
Like butterfly wings,
The snow has gone forever
And it's May,
Yet here I am with you feeling doubt.'

'I'm far away.'

BUTTERFLIES

'I'm not in love with you,
I'm attached to you.'

'Why did you ask me back?'

'I thought it was the best thing to do.'

'What do you mean? You wanted me.'

'There you go again, telling me what I think.'

'That's not thought, that's talking
Like a computer. "The best thing!"
What about love? "Attached!"'

'I'm not in love with you.
When I feel butterflies
In my stomach the way I used to do,
I'll let you know.'

'Is there no in between "in love/attached"?
Can't you just say you love me?
I love you. Sometimes I'm in love with you.'

'I'm not in love with you.'

ALWAYS TWO

'I'm like a computer', you say,
'I have no fears
Whether I live or die.'
On your cheeks are tears,
With the back of your hand you wipe your eye.

'Liar', I say. But like you
I know truth is always two.

'A penny of joy, a penny of pain',
You say. 'At best I amuse myself.
The computer in my brain
Knows what to do.
You would miss me...'

'But wouldn't you miss me?'

'What would I miss?
I wouldn't be there.'

I love you for this and this:
The gloom with your brightness,
The frown with your kiss.

THE HALLOWEEN SMILE

'You have no desire',
I say, and you reply,

'Desire needs space. Would you like this?' –
(You rub against me catlike for a kiss,
With a halloween smile) – 'Your trouble is
You can't stand the truth. Nor can you stand a lie.'

My flesh stands up to you: I agree.
Your truth (or lie?) has got through to me.

AS IF

'It was as if you'd stop breathing
If I didn't let you have me,
So I let you have me.'

'You mean you didn't want it?
Why did you put your hand on my knee?'

'I often put my hand on an arm or a knee.
It's just a gesture, nothing of desire.'

'But when we did it, then you felt the fire.
And afterwards I lay and cried
At being so close to you inside.
You mean you'd truly rather
Not have gulped that seed? I'm the father...'

'It was as if you'd stop breathing
If I didn't. Like our babies teething,
When they were desperate for the breast.'

'I don't blame them. Or myself. You give,
After all. But you know best:
When you put your hand on my knee,
It wasn't that you wanted me.'

'It was as if you'd stop breathing...'

YOU DON'T LOVE ME

'I love you.'

'No. You love what you do
With me. You don't love me.'

'That's not true.'

'You love the pleasure you feel
With me. You don't love me.
In the dark, all cats are grey.'

'What a thing to say.
That's not true.
Cats, or women, are not all the same.'

We lie in the dark. I wait for the sound
I love of the after-midnight train,
Rushing over a mile of ground
Like a football crowd's cheer,
And though I am aglow, I feel pain:

'I do love you…'
(I love your skin. The round
Feel of your breasts and hips drives me mad).
'No one else is here
In my mind.'

And I could add,

'You came! Then I came!
Does this mean nothing to you?'

But I don't. Because I fear
Behind your statement is:
'I don't love you.
I came because you pleased me –
Not for you. For what we do.
I don't love you.'

LINES FROM THE STONE AGE

LINES FROM THE STONE AGE

We lived here first, we of the big bones,
Craggy faces, browridges, high skulls.
We speared eels and salmon with ash harpoons
Edged with tanged flakes of flint, we pulled
Sea bass, blue-and-silver striped, onto the strand
With lines of twisted gut and bone hooks. We culled
Strawberries and bilberries, gathered mast
In oak and hazel woods (we grilled
Fowl on hazel sticks) and by the river
We made our wattle dwellings in this land
We had found our own: our great mother.

Before us came the fish, fowl, songbirds, eagles,
Wolves, foxes, martens, elk, hare, lynx, otter –
The mother's scaly, feathered, furry ones.
And we, the naked, raised our heads
To scan the starry nights for the cold moon,
Mistress of the northrevolving sky,
Of women's changes, briny blood, and tides –
The deathwhite breakers tumbling on the sand,
Eddying the great mouth of our estuary,
Forcing the salt taste upstream to the falls
Where salmon swirled into our withy weirs
And in the rainbow spray, on stepping stones,
We stabbed into the foam with blood-stained spears.

After us the small people, slope skulled,
Narrow headed, conceived in the dark,
The calculating ones who moved great stones,
Smelling of sour milk (we of fish and meat –
Our women's breast-milk smell was honey sweet),
The smoothbrowed, calculating, sacrificing,
Landing on waveless inlets with their cattle,
Driving into the mother's heart, burning
The dead elm trees they'd murdered by ringing bark.
Sacrificing! Why could they not let live?
Naming the mother's rivers after cows
As if her crystal floods were rancid milk,
Building earth mounds in the river bends
With passages to let in the sun's ray,
To catch it like an ox's blood, worshipping
The sun's death and birth, not the moon's way.

After them the broad skulled ones, melters of ore,
Warlike, fort builders – people of things
(Swords, helmets, cloaks, cauldrons, torcs, rings)
And of ranks (farmers, chiefs, praisepoets, kings),
The women not much more than mares they rode:
People of the horse (as the dark ones they enslaved
Were people of the cow – us of the salmon),
Worshippers of neither sun nor moon,
Neither fire nor tide: of thunderbolts
Like their swords, then the dead king on the cross

Invasions from the inundating sea,
Wave upon wave, a flotsam of these others

Who suffocated us just like the sand
That drifted in our dwellings on the wind,
The dunes advancing. We were lost in them,
Taken as their mates, women and men,
Becoming them – their fathers, mothers, children.

We lived here first. Not much of us survives:
A craggy brow here, deep-set eyes there,
Jutting nose, high cheeks, wild curly hair,
Something in the blood, the bone, the mind –
Of all of you. And now this weak hand writes
From one who comes from us, and on starry nights
Comes back to us, the moon above the waves,
Or, with a north wind blowing, by day
Stands at the great waterfall in rainbow spray:
His spear is this poor pencil, and his lines –
Of longing, terror, pride, lust and pain –
Are lines of breakers pounding in his brain.

WATER AND EARTH

I've always said our love was down to earth.
Astrologers agreed, our Moons conjunct in Taurus.
But you wanted more romantic poems.
I could not. All I can write of now
Is you sitting the other day on the beach,
Your blue denim skirt, your knees pulled up,
And me knowing and wanting the inside –
Water and earth, water and earth,
Muddy sand, the flow and ebb of tides
Crawling in the crumbling earth
Of our bodies. This is our romance:
Earth dissolved, in an ancient, pulsing dance.

ISLANDS

Two islands but one country
We lie surrounded by a peaceful sea,
The purple sea of night.

Alpine ridges in the sheets
Are separated by dark straits.

Pacific is the pressing air
Between our bodies lying bare.

When I rise the moon is on its back
Like a silver cup in velvet black.

I cross the reddening water of dawn,
A dead volcano blocks the flaring sun.

The ferry enters a mist of white,
Your island lost to sight.

When sun sets in our country
I return across the peaceful sea,
The purple sea of night.

.

&

Time is unfeeling, not hot, not cold,
Not alive, not dead, but everywhere
Fusing cells, jostling them apart,
Driving us together, shoving us aside,
Indifferent to the weeping from the heart.

Its measured science is without a con:
Never itself withstanding, just its clear
Knowing, pushing blindly – no recall
And no persuading it ever to stop
Its constant restless pro and probing all.

And all we set against it is our skin,
Stretched and battered like a tympanum
By its relentless wave-pulse, so intense
We clutch each other fast as we let go,
All trace in us dissolved of present tense.

Flotsam and jetsam of our bodies drift
Behind us on the sea of memory,
As waking lustrous eyes and tender hands
Form bridges for the new words *you* and *I*,
Our fingers interlaced like ampersands.

ZERO

A zero is a no to time,
A no an O with bounds with rounds.
The time-seed cannot pierce its cell
To swell a ball, since cell is wall
Or nothing, swept by wave or all
Its O shrunk from surrounding what –
Pull / pushed to what is / what is not.

A zero is an O a yes
That opens lips to time's ingress,
Becomes its form, its outer skin
(Pulsating genesis within)
And not a gap, no micro-chasm
With blade-thin space, but tissue slides
And rolls together rippled sides.

The membrane of so-called zero
Holds tubules, vesicles in plasm
Moiled on each other oiled by flow,
Cyclosis of the jism, and spasm:
The outside pushed, the inside pulled,
Both coupled in the yes of time –
The inescapable colloidal slime.

DÁN

Irish *dán* – What is given: gift, fate, poem

A poem is a gift
From me to you,
From you to me:
This circle makes it true.

It is a ring of love
Around us both,
Of golden light
In which we pledge our troth.

It holds our bad and good,
Our dark and bright,
Our life and death,
Our insight and outsight.

Nothing but all it takes,
All you, all me:
Possession makes
Us and the poem free.

MIND

'Man is nothing but his mynd'
Bedingfield's *Cardanus's Comfort*, 1576

Nothing but mind: no, man is more than mind.
And mind creates more than more mind: this flesh,
This mesh of matter matters more than mind.
Through blind convulsions birth and love endure
And lure man on to more and more than mind.
So woman, more than man and more than mind,
Will bind him more than mind to her as more
Is born from this embrace of atoms, more
From the interstices through which mind weaves
Its dance no less than this dance of ourselves
Incarnate, Oh incarnate, through the mind.
Mind, mind the trembling selves we leave behind:
Nothing but mind, nothing is left to mind.

IN GRATITUDE FOR THE GENERAL

The Elect who followed in the General's track,
His last mad rush to gain more territory,
Ran more risks than the bullets at their back:
Not all the villages were pacified.
Angry officials claim them but at night
Shiver inside, playing chess to smother
The clamorous beat of hearts longing for mother.

As leaves vibrate in the bush, birds call,
Or enemy throats, natives' blowpipes avenge
The exemplary corpses newly hung
In the village square to proclaim control:
The villagers remember the General.

He fraternised with some, slept with their women,
Though openly at midday through the square
Would promenade his straight-backed, perfect wife,
Defying every hostile, knowing stare.
Some of the children playing in the mud
Show his characteristic marble eyes
And dominating nose. One broken woman
Still limps from when in drunken despair
He threw her down a high veranda stair.

Officials parrot his ideology.
It is said the Capo's directorial suit,
His deputies' shirts, jackets and ties
Come from the General's trunkful of supplies.

In the city – where he had gone laden with maps
And strange devices, marbled rocks, odd plants,
To promote his finds – accused of playing God,
The General was shot by a firing squad.

The war between the villages and city
Is so old no one knows when it began,
Although the General himself would say
It started with his first rebellion.
Always moving along, he could not stay
In either village or city, each campaign
Would draw him further into new terrain.

The Elect followed his path. The dangers:
Mantraps, crazed loss, disorientation,
Visions, mirages of floating mountains,
Lakes that dimmed to swamps, wrens like condors
Looming with cyclonic shifts of light,
And then the terror of the sudden night.
On the journey no rewards except the greetings
And kind handclasps of passing savages
Who recognised them: in the lakes' mirrors
They looked the same, bronzed and dishevelled,
Lithe as animals, cunning in their eyes.
Until they reached the high frontier, the stars –
As if they entered a new universe.

This, then, is where the General came
On that final survey trip from which he returned

Raving with his caravan of goods.
The Elect can learn from him: not to go back.
Sanity hangs on not trusting old friends,
Not trying to convince: bulldozers rust,
Skeletons in their seats, on the foothill track,
Recalling the final greedy thrust
Of city into new territory,
Using the General's hastily drawn maps,
His converted guerrilla villagers
Fleeing from the cruel pillagers.

Frantic village officials with their bust
Of the General, and their in-house gossip
About the size of his penis, his sudden violence
(They bear proud scars) would shoot the Elect on
sight,
Unknowing that beyond the horizon's haze
Lies the world the General sought. The Elect
Beside the crystal lakes pointed with stars
Draw maps by moonlight and by firelight,
And write accounts of miracles and dangers,
Wondering how to get these to the few,
Disguised as citizens or villagers,
Whose eyes must brighten and whose hearts must
yearn
For these eternal heights of no return.

Sometimes the Elect, disloyal to the General,
Disgusted with the village cults whose message
Crackles on the radio when not jammed

By city static, wish him stuck in hell:
He beat his women but they cherish theirs;
His track sometimes circles back on itself
Where theirs now cuts through rigorously straight;
Their maps are no longer the same, nor is their
thought.
They shun the stagnant lowlands where he fought.

Then in bad times when their supplies run low,
Night chills and loneliness making them crazed,
They yell and quarrel and threaten to throw
Each other off cliff edges, or in fear
Stumble down rock slides, paths collapsing
Under their feet. It seems that their New Age
Is founded on a love infused with rage.

At times they sense the General's eyes in theirs:
It was his restless search that brought them here
To mountain tops so passionately clear.
Sometimes on rocky paths they think they feel
His hand touching a shoulder, and they wheel
To face in ecstasy the midday sky
Where spinning waves, the vortices of time,
Whirl into points of light.

                      Do these create,
Or are they sucked in by, our life and breath?
This sky the General saw when facing death.

PASTORAL

The Dresden shepherd to his shepherdess,
His crook upright beside her flowered hem:
Your eyes reflect the sky. Ah, tenderness
Is due this heart of mine which only beats
For you, my dear. How delicate your cheeks,
Your mouth is like a rose. The budding horns
Nub hard beneath his curled wig as he speaks.

He thinks: *I'll tear the curlicues and flowers,*
I'll blunder through the lacy frills, the pleats
Of your unnecessary satin dress,
I'll tup you in the grass, cover your bleats
With bellows of exemplary fierceness,
I'll concavate my heaving, woolly paunch
Around your jutting, creamy, soft-whorled haunch…

He only thinks. He is a gentleman
Playing at shepherd (or a shepherd playing
At gentleman) and she a lady playing
At shepherdess (or shepherdess at lady) –
More than lusty ram and quivering ewe.

Or could it be that both are something less?
Gentleman, lady; shepherd, shepherdess,
Playing at being more than merely sheep
Counting themselves to death to fall asleep.

MANTIS

To locate the 'ear' responsible, the scientists used a
process of elimination. They removed a mantis's legs
and coated various parts of its body with a heavy
layer of petroleum jelly or melted wax.
                    Science News, 15 February 1986

The praying mantis preyed upon by men:
They stick electrodes in his abdomen,
And by a process of elimination
Submit all six legs to an amputation,
Seal with petroleum each orifice,
And bombard him with ultrasound – all this
To find his single Cyclopean ear,
A breast-groove catching all he needs to hear.

It is the well-known, pitiable fate
Of mantis to be eaten by his mate.
Now there's one more thing for him to pray
For: that death comes the usual way.

TO ENGLAND

1

My only recurring dream: grass, damp grass,
Flowers in stone walls. My dream of England.

There is a ghost in those dreams,
A woman with an alwayschanging face.

Can she be more constant than she seems?
Which is more real? The vision or the place?

2

I cried at pictures of that Northern dale,
Rains of tears swept through me from the fells.
Trapped in a New World, longing for an Old,
The restless dreams came back again,
Of stone walls, and moors where she now walked,
Wraith from the past: I knew it must be her,
For though her face was changing or not seen,
Her name was spoken in my ear by voices
As I followed her bare footprints on the green.

Nostalgia fuelled the quest for a country,
A part of myself I thought I needed to find:
I had never seen the moors that held my mind.
Then, turning a page in a library *Times*:

'The bride wore a dress of wild silk.' (Wild one,
The silk band fell from her unruly hair
The day we climbed the ancient tower stair...)
Satin slippers from flagstones keep her toes,
The tangled bridal wreath confines the rose.

A ghost, a wraith, my lady of the hall,
Protected by guard dogs and the serving men,
I cannot see her form through that stone wall.

3

The stone walls have no doors.
I wander on the darkening moors.
In sweeping rain I cannot see.
No inside country waits for me.
Grass to my knees, slowly sinking
(The dreams were wishful thinking),
I tell myself my love is outside time
As I descend by inches into slime.

4

The ghost turns out to be a witch.
Under her silks, desire's an itch.
The hall's a smart house in town.
On its plaster, tears run down.
At the window is a face
Tortured with sadness, rage, disgrace.
The garden smells of rosemary,
Slugs infest the shrubbery.

AVEBURY

Among the timeless stones what takes the eye
Is a girl on a bicycle –
Pink blouse, and black skirt riding up her thigh –
Pedalling fast
As if in danger in this place,
Through time a-race.

The church clock strikes above the chanting choir
At practice, and the doves inside their cote
Cru-croo-cru, cru-croo-cru, cru-croo-cru,
Then lower – Ooo, Ooo, Ooo – throat to throat.

Impossible to tell which stones, which sheep
Against the downs from far – all seem to sleep,
Until the little ones jostle the big
To suckle and their plangent baas are heard
Quavering through the stilled air of dusk,
Circles dissolve, stones seem to push and shove –
Except the giant ones nothing will move.

Like weeping, laughing, dodderers and crones
Humped or crouching in the grass, the stones
Scarred by cutting flints, eroded, lined,
Holding hands to knobbly chins, must know
More than the visitors who come and go.

As the sun sinks I mount the avenue,
Each stone a foresight for a nimbus flash.

My heart is heavy as the sun's red ball,
For at the top is (nothing?): darkness, pall.

Some stones are coupled: male to female face,
Tall-short, slim-broad – great Mammas and Papas,
Their children straggle after them in lines
Doing what they have been set to do,
Pointing out the way the centuries through.
The living (no more living?) couples pass
Between them, interweaving on the grass,
Hand in hand to watch the red sun set.
These lovers haven't faced each other yet.

In the pub within the ancient ring
Yobs hit the jackpot on the fruit machine,
Neon lights flash, the jukebox flickering
As the pale barmaid hears a goddess sing:
'Taam after taam…'
Outside the plaintive bleating of a lamb:
The dugs are dry.
The dead sun's blood is streaming in the sky
Around the spearpoints of the church's tower.
The darkened stones retain their endless power.

BLACK HILL

HONESTY

The parchment panes of honesty
Reflect the candle-light.
I want to make a vow
To be as straight in future
As I am, naked, now.

Pathways taken in the past
Are lost in tangled brush.
Truth's machete clears them out,
But honesty when cut
And dried relieves no doubt.

Not spectral in translucent pods
My own seed stirs within.
The candle flares to your warm flesh.
Not like this lunar rclic,
Your honesty is fresh.

SOLOMON

We lie upon a hill of bones,
A thin soil over ribs and knees
And skulls from whose gone mouths the moans
Are lost in centuries.

Your cat-loose skin, your silky hips
And thighs, your breasts as in the Song
Of Solomon, your open lips
On mine will not stay long.

Your breath's a mist that fades on glass,
Your lips will fall, your breasts to dust,
Your bones to stones, your hair to grass,
Your blood to earth like rust.

(NO YES)

It is more easy to say no
No yes) than yes in letting go
To you no us no you no I
In this infinity to die
(No yes) another dawn to light
Than melt (no yes) to night.

THE DOUBLE-GOER

Irrational π chose an island.
Rational II (his double-goer) town,
In which to square and multiply himself,
Mirrored with whore-bums, tits, and lip-sticked
mouths,
And after (*une fois philosophe...*) debate,
Horrored by AIDS, clap, herpes, pimp's knife-prick,
Went home (*... deux fois pervers*) to masturbate.

While that absurd, irrational ππ,
Naked in pouring from the ocean rain,
Ate berries: salal-, salmon-, huckle-, black-,
Until his lips were purple with the stain,
Then scrabbling, knuckles skinned, in underbrush
Found tinder, kindling, struck a fire and blew
It high before his grinning face: uprush

Of sparks swirled to fir-tops. *She* appeared,
Her eyes like embers, hair burnished by fire,
Nipples like charcoal on Her smoky skin,
Queen of the night with ππ to dance and spin,
As from Her lightless radiance he, the surd,
Formed circles: from the island out and round
Spread pulses of concentric heat and sound.

π's and his Love's vibrations hummed and blazed
Even through II, the square, only aware
When he awoke under a tree, numb, dazed,
Bemuddied, ashed, beside a smear of tar
Where ravens picked at small splinters of bone
A merciful soft rain was washing white,
Falling through slanted bars of morning light.

AS WE LIKE IT

We live where fragments of the past remain:
Otherwise we're on an endless plain
Under death's white mountain.

By day among the traffic in the street grime
We must work in the world's time,
Our busyness no crime.

At evening along lanes known to Shakespeare,
We walk to have a drink at The Bear,
And know we are somewhere:

Among the forest of Arden's last oaks we have a
sense,
As we like it, of making no pretense
Of other than past tense.

MY FATHER, ST MARKS, ARMAGH

> *'Ni hé Dia na marbh é, ach Dia na mbeo.'*
> *'He is not the God of the dead, but the God*
> *of the living.'*
>
> *Mark XII, 27*

I wonder did you hear the bomb
Whose blast rolled across your tomb.
But ashes are ashes – no ears
Nor eyes, though good for others' tears.

Did the gravelly ground
Reverberating from the sound
Rattle the urn? But you
Can't know or care for anything,
Not even springtime pushing
Leaves out on the lime avenue.
Or can you hear the funeral knells
Through the spire's architraves,
As the occasional others
Join you, your sisters and brothers,
In the untidy graves?

Does the silent ringing
Of lime flowers' golden bells
Carry above the singing
Of choirs racketing in the nave,

And reach across the grave?

Could you have heard the shot,
When a man – some violent thick,
Who knows? – was rendered not?
It floated across the Mall,
Innocuous as the click
Of cricket bat on ball
From the playing field, or 'How's that?'
Yelled out when wickets fall.

Can you hear calling you
The silent ratatatat
Of the lime drumsticks' tattoo?

ATLANTIC

On the golden sands of youth
Where I searched for truth,
Under clouds black with rain
We two walk in pain.

On Sheephaven's glassy brink
Horn Head seems to drink
Like a crouching brontosaur.
In dunes behind the shore
Pink and yellowstriped snails climb
And fall, niched in time.

You say all our emotion
Comes from this ocean.
We're hit by a sudden squall
Whose rain smudges all,
Turning golden sand to black,
Blotting out our track.

Children of the wide Atlantic,
We can become frantic
With gales of rage or fear
Any time of year,
Or be swept by storms of grief
Drenching blade and leaf.

But, head down, soaked, I know
Soon a double rainbow
Will dip like steaming candy
Into a rippled sea

THE POET'S BALL

For Martin Seymour-Smith

'The poet's ball', the leg-break – twist
Of cunning fingers, folded wrist.
Then why do umpires fail to call
Bat out of crease, why shout 'No ball!'
To let the beefy, cocky pricks
Hit the poet's ball for six?
Why does the woman keeping score
Clap her hands and ask for more?

A googly might impress the bitch.
Or poet try another pitch.

BLACK HILL

Along the moorside, scattering sheep,
Clambering over walls of black stone,
Under the lark's twitter in the sky sphere
And the hobby hawk's begging wheep,
I've climbed. I'd thought I was alone.
But *they* were there. They *are* here
On the ridge in a round barrow
Tussocked with grass, crumbling down,
Boulders tumbled into its crown.

I lie on the grass and press my ear
Against a boulder. Dimly I hear:

Who I am you don't want to know.
How it is you don't want to know.

Dimly I see blue eyes scrunched narrow,
White cheeks and forehead, yellow hair.

You don't want to know who I am.
I was killed with me Dad and me Mam.
Death is more than you want to know.
What it's like you don't want to know.

Yellow-haired girl, you don't want to know
How all is changed, nothing is changed.
I lie despairing on this slope.
In this world I find no hope.

Here I am with the whiffling air,
And wheeping hawks, and larks so high
I can't tell where they are in the sky.
No flowers for a grave, the moor is bare.

Draw me a circle on the stone
With your finger, a cross in the circle – so.
And put your lips to the circle – so.
This is my forehead, kiss my forehead
So I can feel that I'm not dead.

I've kissed the cross in the circle – so.
Along the moorside, scattering sheep,
I descend to the hazy valley below.
Three hares start from my track as I go.

Yellow-haired girl asleep in the ground,
Under the grass and stone of your mound –
I don't want to know. You don't want to know.

PILLOW TALK

PILLOW TALK

You sometimes ask, last thing, in bed,
What is the meaning of life?
And I make some answering quip,
Kiss you, snuggle my head
On my duck-down pillow, and sleep.

But last night when I said
I'd like to own one part
Of you, one place at least
(And I didn't mean your heart)
Where I can be a beast
Because you are my wife
And I can call you mine,
You said I was for hire
(Teasing me) to any woman
Who'd pay me in attention.

The pillow talk of concubine
And emperor of China
Was not like this. But now is now,
And, Love, I wish I knew
The meaning of life
For us, me, and you.

NIGHT THOUGHTS

What does not die in us is not alive:
We are doomed to live, not to survive.
And what survives from us as memory
In others is not immortality.
We are no more lasting than bronze crumbling down
To a dull glint in earth's relentless brown.
After all our loveliness, at the limit
We'll end as something very close to shit.

But a poem, once outside me, may survive,
Since, though it is not, it may seem alive.
Is its quietus in its utterance?
Each poem seems its own death sentence,
Pronouncing now at one with then.
But Oh when do we live? When?

Is our view of life merely a wake,
A vee of foam behind us on a lake
We zoom across in a boat drunkenly
Heading for death's black cliff to smash
And leave flotsam and jetsam to wash
To the shore of others' memory?

Can we claim integrity, a whole?
Who perceives the gestalt of our soul?
Are we a series of regressive selves
Imagining from vague receding shelves?
If what will die in us is what's alive,

Then what is dead is all that can survive.

We cultivate finality. The doom
That creeps coldly through us as we say
'*I love you*' reassures us we will die.
'Love' in inverted commas, in the sky
Of a blank page that darkens in the gloom
Of dusk, disappears in night, but day
Reveals new blanks for new 'love'. You and I
Will be long gone, having been alive,
But 'love' ad infinitum will survive.

Words will start again, begin to sprout
From our live mouths. And even if I shout
'*Enough!*' then stop, we won't survive.
What does not die in us is not alive.

FROM DEVON TO THE PACIFIC

The sun rolls down the coomb edge,
Seems to die in pools of red,
Sets here but rises where you rise.

Here all day silvery it shone
On frosted slopes, trees, cob walls, thatch.

As snow melts in your Pacific gloom
And your breath steams in the chilly room,
Before you kindle the breakfast fire
Think of my desire.

Sun melting lies/dies in coomb cleft – is gone.

NO TO NO

O Canada, the band plays
On the sun-deck of the ferry.
Lust like an arrow
Shoots ahead of the prow
Slicing through the sound
Where killer whales prey
On salmon, seal, and otter.

(O of two backs arching
Like killer whales
Leaping, standing
On their tails,
O like parentheses
Face to face around
A soundless sound).

The sea is innocent of slime
And mud, light-speckled
In its postcard sublime
Northwestern setting,
Sun sparkling on the snow
Of the Olympics.

I know
(O of this poem in my head:
The usual compound
Of desire and dread)
I will say No to No.

KEEPSAKES

These are passionate things:
Gifts of knickers and of rings,
A dried quince, a pillow touched with scent,
A letter about my penis and your cunt.
Some might think them obscene. I don't.
They are like magic of a girl child
Who calls to witness under wild
Grey moving skies a boy,
Transfixed, sharing her joy,
Her pink slit: his future home
From which (forbidden thought) he's come.

I leave flowers in a book pressed
(Primrose, harebell), I go dressed
In a ragged workshirt
Spattered with paint and dirt,
An acorn treasured in a pocket,
Coins unspent in a busy wallet
(One pound, one dollar must stay)
A smell of you not washed away,
A bead, a button, leaf or stone
Picked from a certain place and stored
All substitutes for a word:
'Home', 'love', 'come' (to you, to me),
Signs of each unable to flee
The other. Or of having gone
Keeping a sense of one.

REMEMBRANCE SUNDAY 1999, GREAT TEW
For Narcis Comadira

As the poppies spread
In the fields at Great Tew
The dead seem few.

The living on the wold
Are too many and too good
To be death food.

Inside the church is cold,
Pews bare as cattle stalls.
Cracked walls.

Those gone to public ends,
Gentry, soldiers, private friends,
Have their memorials.

Inscriptions carved in brass
Or in marble, caulked with grime,
Blur with time.

Outside, in the grass,
A poppy on a tiny cross.
A card: *DICK*. Loss –

A mother or a wife.
Where is the toxic tree of life,
The yew?

As the poppies spread
In the fields at Great Tew
Many are the dead.

Eye-lidded gloom
In brass or stone-lidded tomb
With endless dread

Is all our doom.

IN BAULK LANE

Three rabbits, one pheasant, eight sheep,
Naked oaks along the field's far edge,
Clumps of primroses in twos and threes.

The rabbits are doing their number:
Tumbling, tearing, leaping head over fluff tail,
Brown ballet dancers. The pheasant plods,
Pauses, struts, pecks into sods.
The sheep don't exactly sleep,
But all but: they stand, they nudge, they graze.

(Where are the lambs to gambol with the rabbits
In the stiff March breeze?)

We look at this stage-set over the hedge,
A stall of green frieze –
Leaflets from the ashes, holly,
And here the black-thorn,
Its white blossom. World reborn.

SPÄTLESE / LATE VINTAGE

Late afternoon on the Weinberg,
Sun going down, not going down,
Edges of emerald vine leaves frosted brown,
I stopped to sample grapes
Swollen so tight when I plucked them they burst.

As I stuffed them into my mouth I felt a thirst
For something more than them. Of course, for you.
I gazed out at villages, each one a 'home' –
Flonheim, Armsheim, Bornheim, Bermersheim –
I hardly knew.

The juice was clear, cool. The taste of wine –
Blauer Portugieser, Spätburgunder, Riesling –
As I licked my fingers made me want to sing.
Then you sang in my ear. I reached the lookout
Facing North towards the Rhine.

The never setting sun, slanting, half closed
My questioning eyes. I swotted flies,
Tried to trace Flonheim's Roman wall,
And couldn't understand. I didn't know
Who you were at all.

You were not from Celt-land, Frank-land, Rome.
But I could feel you in the October sun:
Bright one.

ROGUES AND WHORES

Where on earth is Hand Trough Creek?
Where are Cuckold's Haven,
Clap's Gate Lane, and Gallions Reach?
Names on a map of Dockland,
To you, a rogue, they promise heaven.

Outside St Paul's, gaze
At this puddle in the lap
Of a black marble woman
Reclining. The water glistens.
Let John Donne speak:

Not a minute left to do it
(Repent, he means, not love –
The Dean is not a poet).
Not a minute's sand.
(An hour glass on his pulpit).

His shrouded death-mask listens.
The hour glass
Is just a frozen shape
In a quantum landscape:
Time doesn't pass.

The sermon doesn't teach,
But endures like the walls
Of old St Paul's
And blitzed houses ablaze.

All that moves is mind.

Here, rogue, stand
By the black woman,
Share her daze,
Frozen in the East wind
From Cannon Street.

Out at Cuckold's Haven
Wives spread their legs
To take on the dregs
Of Gallions Reach
And pass on the clap.

Spend all the coins
From a pocket without holes,
Lie in their loins
And on their breasts blubber
In convulsive emotion:

In the life of dove-tailing souls,
A quiver if not of matter
Of, yes, love.
That can prove
White and black, rogues and whores move.

THE HUGGER MUGGER

THE HUGGER MUGGER

The Hugger Mugger is under the bed,
In the top of the wardrobe, behind the door,
Along the walls and across the floor,
He pushes in on my sleeping head,
Big and smelly, smothers my breath,
Blindfolds me, presses to death,
I can't get out from under him.
HELP!
HELP!
I scream but nobody hears
HELP!
HELP!
I call, my voice is dry
I know that I'm about to die,
The Hugger Mugger is on my face!
I heave him off, my blindfold is stuck,
Adhesive, I have to peel and rip
To see if I can give him the slip.

Now YOU are here.
PLEASE! PLEASE!
He's here in the room!
                              He is, you say,
He's here, he's there, he's everywhere
You are. You think he's gone but he's not.
That's it, struggle up and turn on the light,
Short of breath in the dead of the night,
Stagger up to the open window,

Look at your watch, it's ten to two,
The Hugger Mugger is still with you.
His tender fingers ripple your hair,
He leers from behind the easy chair.
Wherever you are, you are in his grip,
You can't escape him, he is your shame,
Out on the prowl under your name,
The side of you you don't want to know,
Your inside turned outside, rampant,
Grimpant, and grinning with rage and fear
As his razor slashes from ear to ear.

You can scream all you want till your voice will crack,
The Hugger Mugger is on your back.
You can cry all you want till the tears run down,
The Hugger Mugger is on your crown.
The Hugger Mugger will sit on your head,
He will bugger you as you lie in bed.
Why, look where he goes! He's under your feet
As you dash to escape him down the street.

Bare-bummed with dangling dick, in a sweat,
As I run I smell a familiar stench.
There he is sitting on a park bench
In the pool of a glow from one street lamp,
And there beside him sits his vamp,
Her lips gape wide in a sickening grin,
She shares with him, she shares his sin –
Her lips are blue, her lipstick is red,
She snuggles down and gives him head,

She sucks and sucks, she licks and licks
Until at the end she sticks and sticks
And he jumps to his feet and runs down the street
Pursued by this shadow who clings and clings
Crooning and muttering ceaseless things.
He pounds her into a pavement crack,
She sinks with a sigh – but she'll be back.

The Hugger Mugger is on me too,
He's here, he's there, whenever he's you:
Sometimes I catch him in my hair –
A trace of slime that sticks on my comb.
I wipe him off with a tissue and throw him
Into the bin. I've got rid of you.
I am dead to you, I am dead to him.
There you go, gloomy and grim
Looking for your next victim.

But clean up your act, stand tall and bare,
Comb the Hugger Mugger out of your hair.
You will sleep on your front, you will sleep on your back
With a smile on your lips, and if I am kind
You will find me beside you, my flesh at your side,
The corrugated soft ridge of my sole
Just touching yours as we spin and glide
Like a sycamore seed through breezy air.
The Hugger Mugger was in your dreams.
Be here in me.
ALL IS WHAT IT SEEMS.

Now is the end of your nightmare.
Now I have you in my care
Clinging to my night-dark hair.

XMAS DAY 2001, DEVON

Death is everywhere – in the gorse preternaturally
Flowering in December, in the slanting
Of the sun across the green-gold coombe.

My love so far over the lavender sea,
I think of doom.

Lichen ochre on church stone, fern blackening,
Shingle on the beach growling,
Beech hedges rusty lines across the hills.

The heart fills, and fills.
The veins empty.

MUMM'S CHAMPAGNE

When you cracked open the Mumm's champagne
To celebrate our first whole night –
In the new sheets you had bought, striped blue and
white –
You didn't know how much pain
Would follow from being together.

But our love has not turned vinegar,
Though it's no longer bubbly – a blood red wine
Pressed from the last grapes of two ageing vines
Whose limbs would have to be snapped
To get them apart.

We have grown around each other, and here
Are the same sheets, the stripes faded and worn,
And a bottle of something more modest than
Mumm's.
The champagne spurts
And though we forget nothing, nothing hurts.

FROM CHAIR TO CHAIR

I sit in your chair and I look at my chair and despair
At the lack of a view of us both, as above in the air
A vee of geese honking veers down to the park and
its lake
And I don't know if ever I'll love you without a mis-
take.
You know what I am but whatever I am is not clear.
All I know in your chair is I wish me in mine and you
here.

Chair is flesh in your language ma Chère, I am able
To envision my body, to see me from you across the
table.
But this is taboo to my mind. I would usually think
It schizoid in a void to see me through your eyes, in
a blink.
(What pain will he cause the next time he moves off
and comes back?)

When I look at my chair opposite, its pressed back is
a rack
Where my body is stretched – seen from you – or
(another view)
I am back in my own self there in that chair and see
you
Bleeding slowly for me – as I bleed for you now:
face to face,
I don't know which way the directions of time or of

space.
As I look at you in my mind are you looking at me?
In a warp of the universe not here or there we
Are two knobs – a tube in between – a dumb-bell
Tumbling over and over it seems between heaven and
hell.

Your email: *I love you very much.* But here in your
chair
With nobody there in my chair my existence is bare
As if I'm alone in a pew in a dusty old church,
Ready to pray you won't stay far off and leave me in
the lurch.

Where is our azimuth? When can we stop
The tumbling? – and still stay connected and drop
As one down to earth and just be you and me
Each in our chair sitting here with the locust tree
And the usual Constable clouds to look at, and we
Both North both South, each an alternating pole
Of a vast rolling world we don't need to control.

SOMETHING LIKE LOVE

Lake Monroe, Indiana

The grass is worn and beaten down
By snow just gone,
Each tree in the wood alone.

We sit, us two,
On a fallen log above a view
Of ice sheets fraying into water.

Gulls shriek
And crows cry out in desperation.
A pair of cardinals flit in a naked oak.

A blue jay picks at the ground,
A party of scuttling killdeers call their names,
A dove goes 'tink tink' like a muted bell.

A long ago hell
Comes to mind, a Spring without promise.
Now there is nothing to miss.

Is this perfection?
Expectation, the ice melting.
Is our long time of despair really over?

We make
Something like love before we fall asleep

And as we awake.

Will this hush
Of nothing happening before the Spring
Tempt these New World birds to sing?

Buds will burst and shoots like arrows leap.
Melting will push
Volumes of sap up through the waiting bush.

We shall make
Something like love again by the shimmering lake.

THE PERMANENT MISSION / DIE STÄNDIGE VERTRETUNG /

1

Blackbirds in a Berlin square
At dusk from bare trees talk
Back and forth as I walk.

Blackbirds talking in my head
Back and forth say I'm dead
Until I hear you say you care.

2

This is separation distress by the book.
Panic: where are you?
(I know very well where you are – not here.)
Loss: on the edge of tears, grief gnaws
At the heart. And fear:
My eyes widening to find a way through
The flickering woods of separation to you.

Take a look
In your own heart's half open book.
Do you miss me too?

3

The sight of golden crocuses by the Spree
Puts a new spring in my tread.
(I had given myself up for dead.)
And although you are far away

I imagine you at the end of a long Allee
And my step quickens. I shall arrive
Sooner or later, alive.

4

I don't want to leave *Die Ständige Vertretung*,
Although I am alone, and no one will come
To meet me here. All is well. After my Weissbier
And lunch I sit happily with a Kirsch and a black
coffee.
If I were on my way I fear
The images would fade in my head
That keep me from going dead.

CHIDDINGLY

You concentrated on hassocks embroidered
By the Women's Institute across the years,
I on an Elizabethan family in alabaster on the wall,
The man lying on his side, cheek on his elbow,
Above his wife on her back, head on her pillow.
A smell of flowers from a wedding festival –
White roses on the pew ends, bouquets of lilies –
Made me think of death and you of life.

Outside from the cricket field the click of bat on ball,
White figures on green, the blue line of the Downs.
This is where my parents used to walk
In time of war. (I hear my father in my talk.)

I shall celebrate our anniversary
Not with lilies: with a red rose on a long stalk,
And on a petal a drop of silver dew.
But now you are gone, I can't deliver it to you.

THE QUIET ROAR

We have always been quiet lovers
Each absorbed in the other
Until at the end a sigh, a cry,
A name, a groan, a moan
Or best of all a quiet roar
Then silence – like a wave on a shore.

THE MEMORY TREE

There's something not quite right about that tree –
The Memory Tree – those names looking down at
me, swinging eerily.
The man who burned to death in his own house,
And the woman he had run off with from his tire-
some spouse,
Then *she* died, and that's why he… or so it's said.
They're not around, mind you, no buried dead.
But you shoulda seen that arrow, it went awry,
Haywire, ricocheting from tree trunks, with a
god-awful dead twang
From the string. I thought it'd bust but the bow was
OK,
Or maybe it was the arrow nock but no bits flew. I let
loose another
At that albino mountain goat, but it missed. And
another.
It missed too. At least I found them. That first one,
I must have searched for it half an hour, in the poison
ivy,
Snapping branches, tripping on lumber trash,
I almost hung myself on a branch. Then I gave up,
Left my arrow as an offering for those dead.
They mayn't be there, but they sure were inside my
head.

I tell you, they spooked me. It took another target
Before I got my aim back: the standing brown bear,

Three arrows like buttons down his chest,
But I doubt they laid those ghosts to rest.
You guys know what they're called, those flowers
That sprung up in the clearing just before you get to the moose,
Like waving mauve carnations? 'Bouncing Bet'.
I'd rather have a Memory Clearing than a Memory Tree,
The dangling wooden names each with a story.
But live flowers are for life, not death, I guess.

ANGEL WINGS

1

Two fallen angels in the snow –
I see them from my window.
Yards apart, at odd angles.
From some disaster in the sky?
Their fused wings glow in the dark.
Nothing to make me cry.

I was both angels. From each,
Tracks lead away. Tomorrow
There will be more snow.

2

As I looked up to the window
And saw you writing at your table
I felt a warm tingling on my back,
As if I were going to sprout
Angel wings and fly to you –
And flap against the pane
I'd try to break through
To you, inscrutable.

But you smiled, waved, I felt the glow
Again where wings burst out.

MISSING NOW AND THEN

If I were to go back to then   barc
With her in summer daisy fields,
I'd miss you! You wouldn't be there!
And though I'd do it again and again
(Being young) as lustful as a ram
(As with you I now less often am)
She would be missing all those other men.

So memories stand in between
The now and what has been.
So now's not now and then's not then,
And I'm not free. Nor you. Nor she.

I miss you horizontally,
And do I miss her vertically?
No, I miss what *was* – pastimes
On grass built over by the years.

And I miss what *is* – you where you are,
Behind your windowpane a tree
That doesn't grow in this country.

THE SLIME-BALL

After shaking hands with this slime-ball
(Being polite as usual),
Walking along Oxford Street
I bent and washed my hand in a dirty puddle.

Dealing with slime
Is difficult: it doesn't quite
Wash off, but the puddle did the trick.
Otherwise I would have been sick.

THE BARN ROOM

The barn room where we played those wind quintets
By Mozart is falling to bits,
The ceiling panels dislodged by racoons –
Eating glue, I suppose – their shits
Dried on the now rotting spruce-plank floor I laid.
The barn is falling down, like us who played
There almost as one.

The clarinet, the flute and oboe,
The horn and bassoon are set aside in dust
Or lost. There is no room for us now.
And we have no need of it: dead or dying
As all things do – even barns, even raccoons.

If I had stayed there, steward of that place,
I could have held back entropy
A while. I would have shot the raccoons, at least:
They would not have had their nocturnal feast
In anything of mine.

It's the dark hair and eyes
Of the clarinettist that worry me, the studiousness
Of the flautist, the joie de vivre of the horn –
All gone. (I don't know where the oboeist is).

But I am here. Perhaps I should take up the bassoon
Again: same fingering as the flute I've set aside,
And the saxophone I played
In the local dance band – a double life
In music! All gone. Too soon.

TWO SONG CYCLES

THE ECHO CYCLE

Song Cycle set by David Jaeger, 2017

WELTSCHMERTZ

Pain of the world – Weltschmertz.
Turning toward extinction
So intense the red
Berry clusters of the rowan,
New paint on the pillar box,
Last geraniums of the year.
All will be leached, all bled –
As from her lovely flesh, this dear
Who walks in joyous pride
As if there were no wintertide.
The world hurts.

ECHO

If you are Echo, I am a wall
To which your voice can call
And be returned but slightly changed,
Not quite itself but rearranged
In newer harmonies. What you will hear
Is not what you might fear.

THE BLACKBIRD IN THE RAIN

The blackbird in the rain at dusk:
I don't know how the drops settle on his wings.
I am lost.
I wish I knew the meaning of things.
I wish I knew whether or not to trust
Myself in my (I think they are) delusions
Of what or who you are –
Or are they illusions?
My own voice from afar

Says to the blackbird as he sings
'I am you are I'.
The rain falls darkening the dying sky.

THE BERSERK BLACKBIRD

Rickety-rackety goes the berserk blackbird,
Riff on riff, perched on the cliff
Of a locust tree, I'm caught
In the torrent and debris of his song,
His notes like jostling boats
As they pour along.
I'd be breathless
If I were he, I almost expect him
To topple head-first to the ground
Killed by his own sound.

THE SOUND OF A SMILE

There are noises at the limits of the ears,
I'm not sure always if imagined or heard.
For example the sound of a smile,
Or the upper harmonics of a third.
The first is an almost silent swish,
The second an almost seen sound.
I can't recreate them as I wish.
They slice across the usual ringing background.
The rustle of the dead in their graves,
The hiss of an anthill that seethes.
The hum of an aurora's waves.
The sough of a baby as it breathes.
These sounds aren't like the chewing of the cud
By a cow in a distant field, which peering
One deduces. I mean a real noise
Out at the edges of my hearing –
Or inside my head – I don't care.
The sound of a smile is surely there –
As much as the harmonics of a third –
As truly heard.

THE SOUND OF THE SOUND

The sound of the wind in the trees, and of the
sound…
Let me explain. We are in a clearing
In the woods – birch, maple, spruce, fir – and the
breeze

Bends and sweeps, twists and turns the trees.
They hiss, rustle, swish with unvoiced sound
(The only voices ours). So far so good:
These arc the sounds of the wood.
But the other sound, from out in the bay
(The sound) - not with us at low tide, a mile away,
Then more like a change in the background:
Not a roar (that cliché) nor the boom
Of waves, it's a steady rushing
As the tide engulfs the sandy, muddy ground.
This is the sound of the sound.

POEMS OF ABSENCE
Song Cycle set by James Moffet, 2019

TRANSATLANTIC

The long howl in the mind
As the traces unwind
At six hundred miles an hour:
You are taken away from me.
My love, all you have done
Remains in me as one
No matter how far
Your body is displaced from me.
I can think myself in you,
Stand where you have stood,
Imagine my heartbeat
Overlaps yours as I set my feet.
The heart you scrawled
In pencil on an envelope
Addressed to me, leaves its trace
On my heart.
Where we were
Is where we are.

WHERE YOU ARE

The birch tree writhing, the cherry wriggling, the
locust trembling
In the breeze of dusk. The evening star.
Opaque clouds in the darkening blue.
I think of you
And where you are.

SLEEPY HEAD

'I always sleep well', you say.
I wish you were here now
In the other half of this bed –
Sleepy head –
But you are far away.

IN ME SOMEWHERE

Every so often I dream of you
And wake up happy (even if things have gone wrong
As things do in dream), since you have been away so
long
And now are with me in bed. I reach out my foot
quite far
In search of yours but your foot is not there
As in my dreams you sometimes are:
That must suffice. Although I cannot bear
Too long an absence, you are in me somewhere.

IN THE AIR

As you have been up in the air
I have been everywhere,
Every room in the house, every corner of the garden,
My longing for you a long thread of love
Stretched at 600 miles an hour.
Does place mean anything?
Sadly, yes.
My guess
At where you are can't be exact.
Though I know where I am in fact.
Sunlight through the window
As I sit in my swivel chair
Writing this to you, I hear
The sound of a plane descending

As you will descend
Four thousand miles from here.
How can it be
That when I woke up this morning
You were lying next to me?

RECIPE

What to do when you are lonely,
And feel about to die?
This is my recipe:
Write an email to your love
And wait for a reply.

READY TO ARM

'Disarmed. Ready to arm.'

Alone with the voice of the burglar alarm
I look out at leaves falling from the birch,
And I feel I've been left in the lurch.
But I'm safe with this voice,
And this is my home by choice.

THE WOOLLEN COAT

You appeared at the edge of a dream,
In your cream woollen coat and black beret,
Standing slightly apart
From a group of people on a hill.
You were standing still.
Were you looking at me?
I was too far away to see.
Then I awoke apart.
Yes, you are too far away.
But I've just seen you there,
And I'm not unhappy as I start
My solitary day.